always kiss me good night

always kiss me good night

Instructions on Raising the Perfect Parent

by

147 kids who know

THREE RIVERS PRESS
NEW YORK

COMPILED BY J. S. SALT

to my parents, who raised me right

Copyright © 1997 by J. S. Salt

Published by Three Rivers Press, New York, New York.
Member of the Crown Publishing Group.

Random House, Inc. New York, Toronto, London, Sydney, Auckland

www.randomhouse.com

THREE RIVERS PRESS is a registered trademark and the Three Rivers Press colophon is a trademark of Random House, Inc.

Printed in the United States of America

Design by Karen Minster

Library of Congress Cataloging-in-Publication Data is available upon request.

ISBN 0-517-88738-X

20   19   18   17   16

contents

acknowledgments

Thank you to the following schools, teachers, parents, and administrators:

Carpenter Avenue School: Heidi Brahms and Jacky Sallow.

Children's Community School: Carol Colone, Joan Lavery, Robyn Lawrence, Shari Esbin Shaw, Ellen Wohlstadter, and Neal Wrightson.

Coeur d'Alene School: Willie Bourgeois, Richard Marcus, Beth Ojena, and Margo Saxton.

Manhattan Academy: Gail Burch, Ken Freeling, Deniese Jaskulsky, and Wendy Shissler.

Kenneth L. Moffet Elementary School: Ricardo Galvan, Carol Hart, Kathleen Hill, Brian Johnson, and Nancy Villalta.

Open Charter School: Grace Arnold, Donna DiBernardo, Susan Epstein, Catherine Johnson, Barbara Moreno, Debbie

Pearlstein, and Judy Utvich.

Palm Crest Elementary School: Terese Caire, Carol Capps, Lauren Diehl, Carolyn Howard, Brent Noyes, Kathleen Salmi, and James Davis, Superintendent.

Playmountain Place School: Judy Arcardi, Cynthia Lamb, Ken Lynch, and Pat Pool.

Roosevelt Elementary School: Pat Samarge, Linda Warner, and Anne Whitley.

Theodore Roosevelt Elementary School: Mary Brewer, Sheryl Hambro, Vonnie Powell, and Catherine Riney.

St. George's Preschool: Linda Bartlett and Barbara Voss.

Windsor Hills Elementary School: Paula Shuman and Gay Square.

Wonderland Avenue Elementary School: Joan Douglas, Ginny Gaimari, and Miriam Mosher.

Yavneh Hebrew Academy: Mike Barron, Lisa Heinrich, Linda Kiefner, Alan Leicht, Beatrice Levavi, Jean Oleson, and Mike Setfel.

Thanks to Celia Kendrick, Karen Langsam, and Jenny Marcus for their guidance. And my greatest appreciation to the experts themselves—the more than one thousand kids who contributed their time, energy, and outstanding insights. A kabillion thanks for showing me the way and letting me share your wisdom with others.

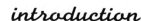

introduction

As my wife and I were about to become parents for the first time, I began to worry: How would we raise this child? How would we know what he needed from us? We were embarking on the most important job of our lives and we didn't have instructions.

Naturally, I looked for books on the subject. But nothing quite fit the bill. Where, I wanted to know, was a simple, user-friendly guide that would give us clear, solid advice—specific things we could do to help our child prosper and thrive.

Being a writer, it didn't take me long to realize: "Here's a book that needs to be written. And, since babies are expensive, why don't I write it?"

But there was a catch. Still a father-to-be, I was hardly what anyone would call an expert. *Then it hit me.* My "experts" would be the kids themselves—people who surely knew what they needed.

In the months that followed, I traveled to fourteen grade schools and met with more than one thousand kids from a variety of ethnic and economic backgrounds. I asked them to write: "If I could tell my parents how to raise me, I'd tell them '_____.'"

Sure, all some kids wanted was their own TV and the freedom to "pour milk down my sister's pants" and "send my brother to Jupiter."

But I also discovered the advice I'd been looking for: kids with greater wisdom than I'd ever imagined; kids who knew what they needed from their family and friends and were clear and straightforward about the caring, guidance, and inspiration they craved.

Very few projects turn out as well as planned. This one, I'll tell you, turned out better.

J. S. Salt

J. S. Salt
Los Angeles, 1997

caring

Encourage me.

Billy, 9

Have convdents in me.

Kelly

───────────✦───────────

beleve that I could acheve
my goels.

AVA Age
11

Listen to me when I am
talking.

Allie

———————☆———————

Don't screem at me
becaus I am small and
I am not pefect.

Jessica

Cheer for me when I get a hit.

David, 10

---⭐---

When I'm crying
say nice things.

Daniela

When I'm down, raise me up.

Eric 10

---⭐---

always have faith in me,
Never get mad at me.

— Robert, 10½

love me like you never loved anyone before.

ayar
10 years old

Never be mean. Always
say "I'm Sorry."

Kathy age 10

☆

complement me.

Brianne 10

try as hard as you can
to be very fair.
thanks

Romy age 9

———— ✦ ————

respet me,
dont egnore me

Schuyler

ELLIOT

make me Be Beautifull.

Jackie

———⭐———

Be there for me.

Barry

Keep your promises better.

Jeanette 10 years old

———————☆———————

Don't leave me in the car
when you go to do stuff.
Stuart, 8

write notes to me ^ on my lunch box napkin.

Jenny
8 years old

Think wehn row were a kid
and Not Yell so much

JOE

———————☆———————

If you get mad at me
remember to forgive me.

Suzanne

snug<u>el</u> <u>me</u> <u>up</u>
<u>in</u> <u>your</u> <u>arm's</u>.

Sasha Age <u>8</u>

love me for what I am.

Ethan 10 yrs. old

───────── ☆ ─────────

Be proud of me even if
I didn't get all the answers
correct.

Sachi
age 10

Don't lie to me.

Marilena 9½

———————⭐———————

dont take me for granted.

Ben 10

sit down and have a
conversation with me.

Kathleen
age 11

say "I love you," once in a while,
not just when I'm leaving for
school.

— Amber — Age — 11

whenever I am in need,
spend all the time you can
with me.

— Leonard, age 8

Hold me when i'm sad.

Melody 9

---⭐--------

give me things to look
forward to.

Rob 10years.

Treat me like you treat your Customers.

Karen Age 10

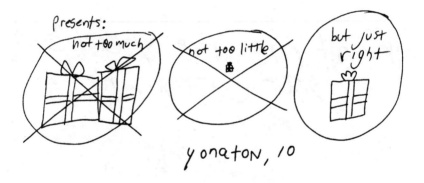

Presents:
not too much
not too little
but just right

yonaton, 10

you must always love me through good times and bad.

Casey
Age 8

―――――――☆―――――――

When I am sick give me room servis. Like bring me food and drinks on a tray.

age 9 Phoebe

lissen to my feellings.

Laramie
age 10

Kiss and hug me when I
am not feeling %100%.

Jessica   age:10

Attend all of my special occasions.

Greg Age 10

---

be proud of my best.

Jessica, age 8¾yrs.

Take care of me till the end of my day.

clara

I love it when I'm considered
as a wonderful kid.

Ryan 10

Keep up the Love

Morty

guidance &
independence

tell me what's right and what
is not.

Tyler 11

Teach me something every
Day.

Eduard

Say "it would help if you do it this
way", instead of "you are doing
it wrong."

Linden

encorrige me to work
on things that I am
not the best at.

LAILA
Age: 10

tell me what I did
right.

Amanda   Age: 10

———————★———————

Help me with stuff I dont Understand.

Erica
Age=11

Don't laugh at me when
I need to ask ?'s.

Julie Age 11½

---☆---

when I have troubles let me
talk to you about it.

Racheli 9 years old

If I get in trouble let me face
the consiquences.

David age 9.

　　　　　If I want to buy
something with my own money let me
buy it because I'm paying for it
not yoae and its going to be mine
not yours.
Katherine 9

STIMULATE MY MIND.

CHRISTOPHER   AGE 8

don't pick out my close.
let me dress the way I want.

Bryna
9 yers

Please don't Kiss me
in front of School.

Britney

52

let me make a mess
when I doing art.
Addison

———————☆———————

Let me play in the Durt
or play in the tree.
Jaclyn

Make me be smarter.

Amanda 9

Let me make decisions that I think would be as good and mabye they would be as good as the decisions that you made for me.

CALEB, 10

Support me.

Curran 12345678910

Help me on my
computer.

Age 9   Celia

help me with my homework.

Casey
Age 8

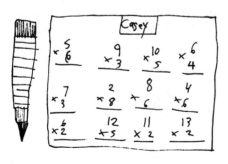

Casey

5 × 6	9 × 3	10 × 5	6 × 4
7 × 3	2 × 8	8 × 6	4 × 6
6 × 2	12 × 5	11 × 2	13 × 2

I want to be in charge
but you still be in charge
because if I grew up
without rules I'd grow
up to be dumb and spoiled.

Christine

HELP ME HAVE FUN!

PAUL, 6

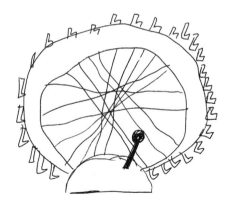

Let me ~~XXXX~~ the Sports I want to
get into

Ben age 10

Let me have my own style.

Stephanie
10 years old

LET ME GET WET IN THE RAIN.

Jessica

Let me go on the Eskalator
that goee up when i'm going
down.

Eric age -9 yrs. old

Let me choose what I want in my lunch.

Steven 9

---☆---

don't try to find out my Secrets.

Stephanie
10 years old

Please don't get in your car and go romeing the streets trying to hunt me down if I'm 2 or 3 minutes late to be home.

Trevor age 12

Dont get mad at me for something
until I keep doing that thing over again.

Jeremy 10 yrs

I like piano, but I would like to stop,
life is good when your a kid so you should
have some fun.

alex 10

treat ME like you would
like to be treated.

Ryan 10 years old

Don't punish me for doing
things by accident.

Aaron 9

More free time!

Don't fill my life up every minute of the day.

—Christine, age 10

Dont make me wear Stupid hats
When it's cold outside.

CeCil 9 yrs.

Help me if I have
problems with my friends.
Alberto 10

———————————⭐———

Interest me in lots of things.
Mendel 11

Don't be so serious with me.

Sarina 9

Teach me to make good and smart judgments.

Matt, 10

Admit that when I do something rude, and then you do the same thing, it's rude too.

Aviva Age 9

Don't get frustrated if I don't understand something.

Kerin, 11

Don't throw away the stuff that
we could put in our recycling bins.

Nicole 10

⭐

Raise me right because
I want to be Someone
in life.

Renadeau
age: 9

Keep on doing what you are doing.

Travrs

family & friends

Let the house be peaceful.

Laura

Let's spend more family, precious time together.

Alanna 9

―――――⭐―――――

Talk to me about your day,

Alison, 10

Give me hugs.

by Christopher 9 age

Give me chores, even if I don't want them.

Jenny, 8

————————⭐————————

When you go on a business trip remember to call me every day.

Andrew

Sometimes can you play with me
instead of saying no?

Frank, 10

———————⭐———————

If you ever have a problem
listen to me. Maybe I can help.

Dylan

Take me places I've never been.

Charles
Age # 10½

Say good bye when you are going somewere.

Jessica

Please learn to respect my friends a little more just as I respect yours.

Megan, 10

Tell me a story about were a child. ^when you

Stephanie

Let my friends come over.

JULLieN AGe 10

In the car if you give them
a chance you can find my
radio stations are as good
as yours.

Leon

Let me have a sleepover.

Jessica 9

Love everyone in our
family a lot!

Dear Richard,
I love everyone in
our family a lot.
I'm sorry I talk
on the phone
so much.

Mom.

Richard   9 Years

respect my
s tuff.

Elyse Agelo

———————☆———————

Don't open my mail.

Mickael (10grs)

come home early

slava

---★---

Stop talking on the Phone
and talk to Me.

Erin 9 years old

come with me to the park.

Andy
10 year old

have a family
meeting for rules.

Brooke age 10

⭐————

Let me have a vote in things
we do together.

Kate 11

Try to give me <u>REASONS</u>
before you send me to my room.

                — stuart

---⭐---

Don't spoil me and then later on yell
at me for being spoiled.

               Ariel   9 yrs old

⭐Brighten up those dull sundays.⭐

ZACHARY Age: 9 1/4

Don't blame me cause
I'm the oldest.

Liz age 10½

———————☆———————

Take me somewhere special once
in a while, by myself, without
my sister.

Vivi 11 years old

sing

Ryan age 9

lagh

Junko
age 9

Be together

Michelle age 10

Play catch
with me.
Walter
age 9

Don't go to work on
weekends.

Elizabeth
9 years old

---

have fun with me every day.

Kerem 8

take me to the movies.

Allison
10 3/4

Take me to the zoo.

Jorge agell

TAKE ME ON CAMPING TRIPS.

Steve AGE#10

Take me out to
a baseball game.

Hannah

---☆---

take me to amusement parks.

Alexander: Age 9

STOP GOING PLACES AND
LEVING ME WITH PEOPLE
I DON'T LIKE .

8 years old | MEGAN

⎯⎯☆⎯⎯

theech me how to
ride my bike.

Armando Age: 8

Don't have Dad work on the house so much.

Jenny 9

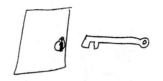

Let me have
Privasey!

Laura

Knock on my door.
Don't just barge in.

— Amber - Age - 11

---★---

when we go out let me do something
that I want to do after you do what
you want to do.

Ariel   9 yrs old

Put good food
that I Like in
the ferge.

10 MATTHEW

Eat dinner with me!

Jessica age 10½

Let me help cook
sometimes.

Brian age: ⑩

buy the kind of ice cream
that I like, not the bad taste
good price kind.

Arthur Age 8

When I come back from school ask
me about my day.

Shawn, 11

———————⭐———————

Try to play foot-ball with me,
dad. Mom is not great.

Jim, 9

like my dogs

Joseph 10

gite me a pet
or a bug.

Jeffrey

take me to where you
grew up.

Rob 10 years

----★----

Tell me stories about my ans-estens.

Bobby 10

Have a family outing every month.

Nigel, 10

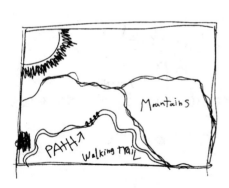

Put your safete belt on
and I will do the same
for my kids.

Rachel
age 10 2 MONTH

Lissen to both sides of a story
when someone gets in truble.

Michael-10

I love it when You give me *Presents*
That are not expected.

Michael age 11

Let me show you all of my creations,

charles g

read to me (even though I can read.)

Amanda 9 yrs.

pick me up and through me in
The Sky.

AGE 9 Maryra

Carry me on
your sholders.

Jules
9 years old.

Let me jump on my bed.

Niki 10

tell me bed time
stories

Mary age 9

Tuck me in.
Shawn

all I need you really already
gave me and that is Love, Careing, and
a roof over my head, and a good family to
Come home to after School.

Amanda 9 yrs.

Never forget to
Kiss me Good Night.

Lauren, 10

have your own advice?

If you have your own instructions for parents—and I'll bet you do—I'd love to know what they are. Who knows? Your words could end up in the next book.

Just write them down (including your name and age) and send them to:

J. S. Salt
4419 Coldwater Canyon Avenue
Suite D
Studio City, CA 91604

Please include your mailing address.